PROVEN
CHARACTER

Praying for Our Children

Phil, 1:9-11
Eph. 6:18

Liz Holtzman

PROVEN CHARACTER

Praying for Our Children

As for me,

far be it from me

that I should sin against the Lord

by failing to *pray* for you.

And I will teach you the way

that is *good* and *right*.

1 Sam. 12:23

LIZ HOLTZMAN

REDEMPTION
P R E S S

Published by Redemption Press, PO Box 427, Enumclaw, WA 98022

Toll Free (844) 2REDEEM (273-3336)

Redemption Press is honored to present this title in partnership with the author. The views expressed or implied in this work are those of the author. Redemption Press provides our imprint seal representing design excellence, creative content, and high quality production.

ISBN 13: 978-1-68314-562-2 (Paperback)
978-1-68314-563-9 (Hard Cover)
978-1-68314-564-6 (ePub)
978-1-68314-565-3 (Mobi)

Library of Congress Catalog Card Number: 2018932866

DEDICATION

To my 6th grade Prayer Committees, I started writing these things down to share with you.

To the women I have prayed with in Moms in Prayer, your faithful prayer support through the years has been invaluable.

TABLE OF CONTENTS

ACKNOWLEDGEMENTS

I am deeply grateful to the team at Redemption Press who have helped make this book possible. I am particularly grateful to my project manager Kate Myers, my editor Hannah Smith, and my cover designer Maryna Zhukova.

My friend, Lisa Dineen, provided invaluable feedback and comments on the appendix material. Thank you to Rebecca and Jon Berry for taking my picture for the back cover. Thank you to my husband, Jim, who helped me create a website and to Niki Manbeck who helped me join the world of Facebook. I am grateful to my family and friends who encouraged and supported me through this adventure of publishing a book.

I am thankful for the privilege of serving a noble mission at The Bear Creek School to help students become all God intends. I am most grateful, to my Lord and Savior, whose call to intercession has deepened and strengthened my faith and our relationship.

FOREWORD

During my first year of teaching at The Bear Creek School in 1999, I had the pleasure of working with Liz's son for third grade. Not only did I enjoy getting to know her family, I also was on the receiving end of her tireless prayers for me and my young family. From the very beginning, and all through the years that I have known her, Liz has been a faithful participant and leader of the Moms in Prayer group at Bear Creek. Her prayer ministry has expanded through the years. Liz takes the time to systematically pray for each teacher at the school. She leads the Prayer Leadership Group for grade six. Under her care, Liz's students learn how to best approach prayer, taking time to thank God and give Him glory. She devotes countless hours to mentoring parents, teachers, and students in developing a thoughtful approach to prayer. Liz even created a prayer room at the school. Its walls are covered with prayers and inspirational verses.

We have all come to depend on Liz for her humble and intentional approach to prayer. We know that we can depend on her to stand in the gap and to truly be a prayer warrior. I will always cherish the written prayers

Liz has provided for me over the years. What a treasure to see her vision of sharing her prayers realized in the publication of this book. This is sure to be a gift to many!

Jenn McDonough
Early Middle School Division Head
Middle School Division Head
The Bear Creek School
Redmond, WA

HOW TO USE
THIS BOOK

The school where I work gives out character awards to each of our students at the end of the school year. The character traits used in this book of prayers were gleaned from the list of awards given to our students. I have written thirty-one scripture inspired prayers that can be used to systematically pray for these traits to develop in the lives of your children or students.

Each trait is accompanied by selected quotes from scripture related to the character trait. Under each prayer you will find a complete list of the scriptures referenced for further consideration. I find reviewing and meditating on them helps influence my thought life. The reminder and affirmation of the Truth deepens my knowledge of God and helps me take captive every thought to make it obedient to Christ. (2 Cor. 10:3-5)

I suggest starting your time of prayer with a time of praise to our Lord, for who He is and what He has done for us. As you are drawn into His presence through worship, have a quiet moment of confession. Thank Him for His blessings and begin your time of intercession using one the prayers for character. You may want to expand your prayer to include specific needs of your child.

There is an appendix with some commentary on prayer and tips on how to do it powerfully and effectively. The role and purpose of each part of a common model for prayer are discussed. In addition, some other pertinent tips and encouragement are shared.

"Our children, created in the image of God, are worthy of the sacrifices demanded by faithful and consistent prayer."[1]

"Arise, cry out in the night, as the watches of the night begin; pour out your heart like water in the presence of the Lord. Lift up your hands to him for the lives of your children." Lamentations 2:19

INTRODUCTION

When I was on a tour of the new building recently built by the school where I work, the Headmaster described the plans for how several rooms were to be used. He concluded their purposes would not be accomplished if we did not make a space for them to happen. The truth of those statements resonates within me as a physical and spiritual reality.

Every aspect of our lives has both a physical and spiritual dimension. Our impact in the physical realm is essential, but limited by time and space. Our influence in the spiritual realm is defined by our knowledge of "His incomparably great power for us who believe. That power is the same as the mighty strength he exerted when he raised Christ from the dead and seated him at his right hand in the heavenly realms." (Eph. 1:19-20 NIV).

Paul calls us to take advantage of that power in two ways in Ephesians 6:10-18. We are to stand firm and put on the full armor of God, so we can take our stand against the enemy's schemes. We are also to pray in the Spirit on all occasions with all kinds of prayers and requests. Because of Jesus' victory over death, we have power in the spiritual realm to stand firm and silence the enemy of our souls. We also have the freedom to invite the Holy Spirit's work on our behalf using the Truths found in scripture. Through prayer we can clean up and influence the spiritual environment in which we and our children make our free will choices. Those choices reflect the character that flows from our hearts. In the same way we created physical space for God's work in our school community, our faithful prayers create spiritual "space" for God to accomplish His purposes in our lives and the lives of our children.

How This Book Came to Be

I lead several prayer meetings a week at the school where I work. I pray with students, teachers, parents, and administrators. I developed a love for writing prayers because more and more, I was writing prayers in emails and devotions. Then, I began to write prayers and print them on cards in an effort to help those who might feel uncomfortable with spontaneous prayer. Whenever I used them, I received frequent requests for copies of my written prayers. Thus, was born the idea to gather the prayers for character together into a book. It just so happened, (if you believe in coincidences, which I don't :-) I wrote thirty-one character prayers. It wasn't until I began to put them together in a book that the light went on in my head and I realized I had one for every day of a month.

The prayers in this book were written to help parents and teachers pray for character development in their students. It is the mission of our school to help our students become all God intends them to be. We wish to see them rooted and established in Him, prepared to accomplish all the good works He has prepared for them to do. Part of how that mission is accomplished is to help our students develop proven character, through perseverance, so they may become mature and complete, not lacking anything. We cannot force character upon them, but through prayer we can silence the enemy and invite the Holy Spirit's influence using the Truths of God's Word.

It is my hope you will use these prayers to pray daily for your children and yourselves. However, whatever way you choose to use them, I know your prayers will be powerful and effective to create "spiritual space" for God's work to be accomplished.

CHARACTER PRAYERS

Therefore, having been justified by *faith*
we have peace with God through
our Lord Jesus Christ, through
whom also we have obtained our introduction
by faith into this grace in which we stand.

We exult in the *hope* of the glory of God.

And not only this, but we also exult in our tribulations,
knowing that tribulation brings about
perseverance.

And perseverance brings about

proven character,

and proven character, *hope;*
and hope does not disappoint, because the love of God has
been poured out within our hearts through the Holy Spirit
who was given to us.

(Rom. 5:1-5 NASB)

19

ATTENTIVENESS

L ord Jesus, Your Word is truth. Help _____ to pay attention to what You say in Your Word so she(he) may grow in her(his) knowledge of You and Your ways.

May _____ recognize Your direction for how she(he) should live. May her(his) careful attention to Your commands bring her(him) peace and well-being. Help her(him) to listen carefully and be observant, so she(he) may guard her(his) heart and maintain discretion.

Help her(him) respect and pay attention to wise people so she(he) may gain knowledge. May _____ consider the blameless and observe the upright. May _____ consider the outcome of their way of life and imitate their faith. Amen

Scriptures referenced:
Ps. 37:37; Ps. 119:14-16; Prov. 4:20-23; Prov. 5:1-2; Prov. 21:11; Prov. 24:32; Is. 48:17-18; Heb. 13:7

Psalm 37:37

Consider the blameless, observe the upright; a future awaits those who seek peace.

Proverbs 5:1-2

My son, pay attention to my wisdom, turn your ear to my words of insight, that you may maintain discretion and your lips may preserve knowledge.

2 Timothy 3:16

All Scripture is God-breathed and is useful for teaching, rebuking, correcting and training in righteousness,

BOLDNESS

Lord Jesus, there are many things in our world that threaten to undermine our faith and our witness. Guard _____'s heart so she(he) may be filled with confidence through the Holy Spirit and speak the Word of God boldly.

When she(he) feels afraid or weak, may she(he) call to You and be emboldened to listen to Your Word and do what it says. Amen

Scriptures referenced:

Ps. 138:3; Prov. 28:1; Acts 4:29-31; James 1:22-25

Psalm 138:3

When I called, you answered me; you greatly emboldened me.

Proverbs 28:1

The wicked flee though no one pursues, but the righteous are as bold as a lion.

Acts 4:29, 31

Now, Lord, consider their threats and enable your servants to speak your word with great boldness. After they prayed, the place where they were meeting was shaken. And they were all filled with the Holy Spirit and spoke the word of God boldly.

COMPASSION

L ord, You are a compassionate and gracious God. You show mercy, abounding love, and faithfulness to those who fear You. Help _____ to clothe herself(himself) with compassion, kindness, humility, gentleness, and patience.

Help her(him) appreciate the compassion You have shown her(him). May her(his) appreciation of Your compassion motivate her(him) to humbly forgive and treat others with compassion.

Give her(him) an open heart so she(he) can show Your love to those who suffer and are in need. Amen

Scriptures referenced:
Ps. 86:15; Ps. 103:13; Micah 6:8; Zech. 7:9; Eph. 4:32; Col. 3:12-14; 1 Pet. 3:8

Zechariah 7:9
"This is what the LORD Almighty said: 'Administer true justice; show mercy and compassion to one another.'

Ephesians 4:32
Be kind and compassionate to one another, forgiving each other, just as in Christ God forgave you.

1 Peter 3:8
Finally, all of you, be like-minded, be sympathetic, love one another, be compassionate and humble.

Contentment

L ord, You are able to provide all we need physically, emotionally, and spiritually. You will never leave or forsake us. Help _____ learn to be content in any and every situation.

Help _____ to be content with what she(he) has and who she(he) is. Help _____ know You are her(his) Helper and will provide the strength needed to obey and serve with contentment.

Comparison can so often lead to discontent. Guard _____'s heart from being envious. Help _____ test her(his) own actions so she(he) can take pride in herself(himself) without comparing herself(himself) to someone else. Amen

Scriptures referenced:
Job 36:11; Prov. 14:30; Prov. 23:17; Gal. 6:4; Phil. 4:11-13; 1 Tim. 6:6-7; Heb. 13:5-6

Job 36:11
If they obey and serve him, they will spend the rest of their days in prosperity and their years in contentment.

1 Timothy 6:6-7
But godliness with contentment is great gain. For we brought nothing into the world, and we can take nothing out of it.

Hebrews 13:5
Keep your lives free from the love of money and be content with what you have, because God has said, "Never will I leave you; never will I forsake you."

COURAGE

L ord, _____ is Your handiwork. You have created good work for her(him) to do. Help _____ to be strong and courageous and do the work.

Help _____ to stand firm in her(his) faith and be on guard against the enemy's efforts to undermine the accomplishment of Your purposes in her(his) life.

May _____ not be afraid or discouraged because you will be with her(him) wherever she(he) goes. You will never fail or forsake her(him).

May _____ place her(his) trust in You in all situations and do everything in love. Amen

Scriptures referenced:
Deut. 31:6; Josh. 1:6-7,9; 1 Chron. 28:20; 1 Cor. 16:13-14

Deuteronomy 31:6

Be strong and courageous. Do not be afraid or terrified because of them, for the LORD your God goes with you; he will never leave you nor forsake you."

1 Chronicles 28:20

David also said to Solomon his son, "Be strong and courageous, and do the work. Do not be afraid or discouraged, for the LORD God, my God, is with you. He will not fail you or forsake you until all the work for the service of the temple of the LORD is finished."

1 Corinthians 16:13-14

Be on your guard; stand firm in the faith; be courageous; be strong. Do everything in love.

CREATIVE

L ord, we only need to look around our world to recognize how creative You are. The wonders of Your creation show how innovative and playful You can be.

Because _____ is created in Your image, she(he) shares in the ability to create, imagine, and bring a unique perspective to an idea or problem. Help _____ to embrace that part of how You created her(him).

Help _____ do all things well and artistically, according to the talents You have given her(him). May she(he) create and produce with a purpose. Amen

Scriptures referenced:
Gen. 1:27; Ex. 31:3-6; Ex. 35:10,30-31; 1 Chron. 28:21; 1 Chron. 25:6-7

Genesis 1:27
So God created mankind in his own image, in the image of God he created them; male and female he created them.

Exodus 31:3-5
And I have filled him with the Spirit of God, with wisdom, with understanding, with knowledge and with all kinds of skills— to make artistic designs for work in gold, silver and bronze, to cut and set stones, to work in wood, and to engage in all kinds of crafts.

DILIGENT

Lord, you have blessed _____ with gifts and talents. Help _____ to be wholly committed to and persistent in developing and using those gifts and talents.

May _____ make plans that through diligence, lead to what she(he) hopes for being fully realized.

May _____ not fall into lazy habits, but be diligent in her(his) work and her(his) service of others. Amen

Scriptures referenced:
Prov. 10:4; Prov. 12:24,27; Prov. 13:4; Prov. 21:5; Rom. 12:6-8; 1 Tim. 4:14-15; Heb. 6:10-12

1 Timothy 4:14-15
Do not neglect your gift… Be diligent in these matters; give yourself wholly to them, so that everyone may see your progress.

Hebrews 6:10-12
God is not unjust; he will not forget your work and the love you have shown him as you have helped his people and continue to help them. We want each of you to show this same diligence to the very end, so that what you hope for may be fully realized. We do not want you to become lazy, but to imitate those who through faith and patience inherit what has been promised.

DISCERNMENT

L ord, give _____ a discerning heart so she(he) will be able to distinguish between right and wrong.

Help _____ not judge others solely based on appearances but on their hearts.

Give _____ a heart that seeks knowledge, is responsive to correction, and listens to wise guidance.

Give _____ insight to be able to understand Your Word and discern what is best. Amen

Scriptures referenced:
1 Kings 3:9; 1 Sam. 16:7; Ps. 119:125; Prov. 1:5; Prov. 15:14; Prov. 17:10; Prov. 18:15; Phil. 1:9-11

Psalm 119:125

I am your servant; give me discernment that I may understand your statutes.

Proverbs 18:15

The heart of the discerning acquires knowledge, for the ears of the wise seek it out.

Philippians 1:9-10

And this is my prayer: that your love may abound more and more in knowledge and depth of insight, so that you may be able to discern what is best and may be pure and blameless for the day of Christ,

ENCOURAGEMENT

Lord, help _____ to find encouragement in Your Word that provides hope. Encourage _____ to have the same attitude towards others You have toward us.

Bring people into _____'s life who encourage her(him) to be self-controlled, teach her(him) sound doctrine, and set an example by doing what is good.

May daily encouragement protect her(his) heart from becoming hardened by sin and enable her(him) to live in peace.

Help _____ to encourage others and build them up. Amen

Scriptures referenced:
Rom. 15:4-6; 2 Cor. 13:11; 1 Thess. 5:11; Titus 1:9; Titus 2:6-8,15; Heb. 3:13

2 Corinthians 13:11

Finally, brothers and sisters, rejoice! Strive for full restoration, encourage one another, be of one mind, live in peace. And the God of love and peace will be with you.

1 Thessalonians 5:11

Therefore, encourage one another and build each other up, just as in fact you are doing.

Hebrews 3:13

But encourage one another daily, as long as it is called "Today," so that none of you may be hardened by sin's deceitfulness.

ENDURANCE

May _____ have great endurance and patience. Let _____ not become weary in doing good, for at the proper time she(he) will reap a harvest if she(he) does not give up.

Let nothing move _____ so she(he) can always give herself(himself) fully to the work of the Lord, because she(he) knows her(his) labor in the Lord is not in vain.

Help _____ to hold fast to the teaching she(he) has received about You.

May _____ fight the good fight, finish the race, and keep the faith. Amen

Scriptures referenced:
Matt. 24:12-13; Acts 20:24; 1 Cor. 15:58; Gal. 6:9; Col. 1:9-11; 2 Thess. 2:15; 2 Tim. 4:7

1 Corinthians 15:58
Therefore, my dear brothers and sisters, stand firm. Let nothing move you. Always give yourselves fully to the work of the Lord, because you know that your labor in the Lord is not in vain.

Galatians 6:9
Let us not become weary in doing good, for at the proper time we will reap a harvest if we do not give up.

2 Thessalonians 2:15
So then, brothers and sisters, stand firm and hold fast to the teachings we passed on to you, whether by word of mouth or by letter.

ENTHUSIASM

L ord, may _____ eagerly seek You and desire the gifts You give. May _____ never be lacking in zeal.

Give _____ wisdom to discern what activities serve a good purpose. Then, help her(him) eagerly work until the job is finished.

May _____ be eager to serve You, joyful in hope, patient in affliction, and faithful in prayer. Amen

Scriptures referenced:
2 Chron. 15:15; Prov. 23:17-18; Rom. 12:9-12; 1 Cor. 12:31; 2 Cor. 8:11; Gal. 4:18

Romans 12:9-12

Love must be sincere. Hate what is evil; cling to what is good. Be devoted to one another in love. Honor one another above yourselves. Never be lacking in zeal, but keep your spiritual fervor, serving the Lord. Be joyful in hope, patient in affliction, faithful in prayer.

2 Corinthians 8:11

Now finish the work, so that your eager willingness to do it may be matched by your completion of it, according to your means.

Galatians 4:18

It is fine to be zealous, provided the purpose is good, and to be so always, not just when I am with you.

FAITHFULNESS

May _____ put her(his) full and complete faith in You as her(his) Lord and Savior.

May _____ hold unswervingly to the hope she(he) has in You because You are faithful.

May _____ be a faithful steward of the grace and gifts she(he) receives from You, using them to serve others.

May _____ be faithful to not just know the truth, but to walk in it. Amen

Scriptures referenced:
Heb. 10:23; 1 Pet. 4:10; 3 John 1:3; Jam. 1:22

Hebrews 10:23
Let us hold unswervingly to the hope we profess, for he who promised is faithful.

1 Peter 4:10
Each of you should use whatever gift you have received to serve others, as faithful stewards of God's grace in its various forms.

3 John 1:3
It gave me great joy when some believers came and testified about your faithfulness to the truth, telling how you continue to walk in it.

GENEROSITY

L ord, help _____ to be generous and willing to share, and to do so without a grudging heart.

May _____ sow generously, giving of herself(himself) and her(his) resources willingly and with honest intent.

Help _____ to not be arrogant or put her(his) hope in wealth.

May _____ be rich in good deeds and take hold of the life that is truly life. Amen

Scriptures referenced:
Deut. 15:10; 1 Chron. 29:14,17; Ps. 37:21; Prov. 11:24-25; Prov. 21:25-26; Prov. 22:9; 2 Cor. 9:6; 1 Tim. 6:17-19

Deuteronomy 15:10
Give generously to them and do so without a grudging heart; then because of this the LORD your God will bless you in all your work and in everything you put your hand to.

2 Corinthians 9:6
Remember this: Whoever sows sparingly will also reap sparingly, and whoever sows generously will also reap generously.

1 Timothy 6:17-19
Command those who are rich in this present world not to be arrogant nor to put their hope in wealth, which is so uncertain, but to put their hope in God, who richly provides us with everything for our enjoyment. Command them to do good, to be rich in good deeds, and to be generous and willing to share. In this way, they will lay up treasure for themselves as a firm foundation for the coming age, so that they may take hold of the life that is truly life.

GENTLENESS

Lord, may _____ have a humble, gentle, and quiet spirit that is evident to all.

May _____ have the patience and self-control to give a gentle answer in tense situations.

May _____ be prepared to stand firm and give the reason for the hope she(he) has in You with gentleness and respect.

May _____'s gentleness be demonstrated in _____'s loving, encouraging, and compassionate care for others. Amen

Scriptures referenced:
Prov. 15:1; Gal. 5:22-23; Eph. 4:2; Phil. 4:5; Col. 3:12; 1 Tim. 6:11; Titus 3:1-2;1 Peter 3:3-4; 1 Peter 3:15-16

Ephesians 4:2
Be completely humble and gentle; be patient, bearing with one another in love.

Philippians 4:5
Let your gentleness be evident to all. The Lord is near.

1 Peter 3:15-16
But in your hearts revere Christ as Lord. Always be prepared to give an answer to everyone who asks you to give the reason for the hope that you have. But do this with gentleness and respect.

HONESTY

L ord, help _____ to keep from telling lies. Protect _____ from being influenced by the lies of others.

Strengthen _____'s commitment to the truth so she(he) will not exchange the truth about You for a lie.

May _____ not let any unwholesome talk come out of her(his) mouth, but only what is helpful for building others up according to their needs, that it may benefit those who listen. Amen

Scriptures referenced:
Ps. 34:13; Ps. 144:11; Prov. 16:13; Prov. 24:26; Rom. 1:25; Eph. 4:25; Eph. 4:29; Col. 3:8-10

Psalm 34:13

Keep your tongue from evil and your lips from telling lies.

Romans 1:25

They exchanged the truth about God for a lie, and worshiped and served created things rather than the Creator—who is forever praised. Amen.

Ephesians 4:29

Do not let any unwholesome talk come out of your mouths, but only what is helpful for building others up according to their needs, that it may benefit those who listen.

HUMILITY

Lord, may _____ be completely humble and gentle. Thank You that You guide the humble in what is right and teach them Your way.

May _____ show the wisdom derived from humility by how she(he) lives her(his) life.

May _____ do nothing out of selfish ambition or vain conceit. Rather, in humility may _____ be patient and value others above herself(himself). Amen

Scriptures referenced:
Ps. 25:9; Prov. 11:2; Matt. 23:12; Eph. 4:2; Phil. 2:3; Col. 3:12; 1 Pet. 5:5-6; James 3:13

Psalm 25:9
He guides the humble in what is right and teaches them his way.

Ephesians 4:2
Be completely humble and gentle; be patient, bearing with one another in love.

Philippians 2:3
Do nothing out of selfish ambition or vain conceit. Rather, in humility, value others above yourselves,

INTEGRITY

Lord, you test the heart and are pleased with integrity. Help _____ walk before You faithfully with integrity of heart and uprightness.

May _____'s integrity be based not on worldly wisdom, but on God's grace.

May _____'s integrity guide her(his) actions. May her(his) integrity be evident in her(his) seriousness and soundness of speech, so that she(he) need not be ashamed.

May integrity protect _____ and keep her(him) safe because her(his) hope is in you. Amen

Scriptures referenced:
1 Kings 9:4-5; 1 Chron. 29:17; Ps. 25:21; Prov. 10:9; Prov. 11:3; Prov. 13:6; Prov. 28:18, 2 Cor. 1:12; Titus 2:7-8

1 Chronicles 29:17

I know, my God, that you test the heart and are pleased with integrity. All these things I have given willingly and with honest intent.

Psalm 25:21

May integrity and uprightness protect me, because my hope, LORD, is in you.

Titus 2:7-8

In everything set them an example by doing what is good. In your teaching show integrity, seriousness and soundness of speech that cannot be condemned, so that those who oppose you may be ashamed because they have nothing bad to say about us.

JOYFULNESS

L ord, may _____ be filled with joy in Your presence
and through Your Word.

May _____ serve You joyfully and gladly in times
of prosperity and in times of difficulty.

Create a pure heart within _____ so she(he) may
find strength and know joy and peace in You.

Lord, be _____'s strength and shield. May _____
be joyful in hope, patient in affliction, and faithful in
prayer as she(he) puts her(his) trust in You. Amen

Scriptures referenced:
Ps. 16:11; Ps. 28:7; Ps. 51:10-13; Hab. 3:17-18; Rom. 12:12;
Rom. 15:13; Gal. 5:22-23

Psalm 16:11

You make known to me the path of life; you will fill me with joy in your presence, with eternal pleasures at your right hand.

Romans 12:12

Be joyful in hope, patient in affliction, faithful in prayer.

Romans 15:13

May the God of hope fill you with all joy and peace as you trust in him, so that you may overflow with hope by the power of the Holy Spirit.

KINDNESS

Lord, may _____ be kind and compassionate to others, forgiving others, just as You forgave her(him).

Help _____ resist being quarrelsome and quickly let go of feelings of resentment that would keep her(him) from showing kindness to others.

Holy Spirit bear fruit in _____'s life so she(he) may speak kind words of encouragement to everyone. Amen

Scriptures referenced:
Prov. 11:17; Prov. 12:25; Prov. 14:21; Eph. 4:32; Col. 3:12; 2 Tim. 2:24; Gal. 5:22-23

Proverbs 12:25
Anxiety weighs down the heart, but a kind word cheers it up.

Ephesians 4:32
Be kind and compassionate to one another, forgiving each other, just as in Christ, God forgave you.

Colossians 3:12
Therefore, as God's chosen people, holy and dearly loved, clothe yourselves with compassion, kindness, humility, gentleness, and patience.

LEADERSHIP

L ord, help _____ to follow Your example and walk in
the way of love. May _____ take note and imitate
those who walk faithfully in Your ways. Help _____ to
not let anyone or anything lead her(him) astray. May
_____ set an example for others in speech, in conduct,
in love, in faith and in purity.

May _____ be eager and willing to serve and lead
with integrity of heart and great skill.

May _____ make every effort to do what leads to
peace and to mutual edification, judging fairly, and
speaking up for the rights and needs of others. Amen

Scriptures referenced:
Ps. 78:72; Prov.19:23; Matt. 20:25-28; Rom. 14:19; Eph. 5:1-2;
1 Tim. 4:12; Heb. 13:7; 1 Pet. 5:2-3; 1 John 3:7

Romans 14:19
Let us therefore make every effort to do what leads to peace and to mutual edification.

1 Timothy 4:12
Don't let anyone look down on you because you are young, but set an example for the believers in speech, in conduct, in love, in faith, and in purity.

Hebrews 13:7
Remember your leaders, who spoke the word of God to you. Consider the outcome of their way of life and imitate their faith.

LOVE

May _____'s love abound more and more in knowledge and depth of insight, so she(he) may be able to discern what is best and may be pure and blameless for the day of Christ, filled with the fruit of righteousness.

May _____ love the truth. May that love of the truth result in a pure heart, a good conscience, and a sincere faith. May _____ walk in obedience to Your commands and love not only with words but also with actions and in truth.

Holy Spirit fill _____ with power, love, and self-discipline. Thank You that love has the power to cover over a multitude of sins. Amen

Scriptures referenced:
1 Cor. 13:4-7; Phil. 1:9-11; 1 Thess. 1:3; 2 Thess. 2:10;1 Tim. 1:5; 2 Tim. 1:7; 1 Pet. 4:8; 1 John 3:18, 5:3; 2 John 1:6; Jude1:20-21

1 Timothy 1:5

The goal of this command is love, which comes from a pure heart and a good conscience and a sincere faith.

2 Timothy 1:7

For the Spirit God gave us does not make us timid, but gives us power, love and self-discipline.

1 John 3:18

Dear children, let us not love with words or speech but with actions and in truth.

OBEDIENCE

Lord, Your love and blessing is with those who fear You, with those who keep Your covenant and remember to obey Your precepts. May _____'s love for You be made complete by her(his) obedience to Your Word.

Give _____ understanding and wisdom, so she(he) may know the proper time and way to keep Your commandments and obey them with all her(his) heart.

May _____'s obedience result in sincere deep love for others that comes from the heart. Amen

Scriptures referenced:
Ecc. 8:5; Ps. 103:17-18; Ps. 119:34; Ps. 128:1; Luke 11:28; John 14:23; 1 Peter 1:22; 1 John 2:5

Psalm 128:1
Blessed are all who fear the LORD, who walk in obedience to him.

Luke 11:28
He replied, "Blessed rather are those who hear the word of God and obey it."

1 John 2:5
But if anyone obeys his word, love for God is truly made complete in them. This is how we know we are in him:

PATIENCE

L ord, may _____ be filled with knowledge of Your will through all the wisdom and understanding the Spirit gives, so she(he) may have great endurance and patience.

May _____ encourage the disheartened, help the weak, give careful instruction, and be patient with everyone. Protect _____ from being quick or hot tempered, stirring up quarrels, and foolish behavior.

May _____ wait patiently for You and grow in wisdom and understanding. Amen

Scriptures referenced:
Ps. 37:7; Ps. 40:1; Prov. 14:29; Prov. 15:18; Prov. 16:32; Rom. 8:25; Col. 1:9-11; Col. 3:12; 1 Thess. 5:14; 2 Tim. 4:2; James 5:7-8

Colossians 1:9-11

We continually ask God to fill you with the knowledge of his will through all the wisdom and understanding that the Spirit gives, so that you may live a life worthy of the Lord and please him in every way: bearing fruit in every good work, growing in the knowledge of God, being strengthened with all power according to his glorious might so that you may have great endurance and patience.

1 Thessalonians 5:14

And we urge you, brothers and sisters, warn those who are idle and disruptive, encourage the disheartened, help the weak, be patient with everyone.

PERSEVERANCE

May _____ run with perseverance the race You marked out for her(him).

May _____ persevere in practicing the gifts You have given her(him) and in obeying Your commands, in good times and bad, so she(he) develops proven character.

Let perseverance finish its work so _____ may be mature and complete, not lacking anything. Amen

Scriptures referenced:
Rom. 5:1-4; 1 Tim. 4:14-16; Heb. 10:36; Heb. 12:1; James 1:2-5, James 1:12

Hebrews 10:36

You need to persevere so that when you have done the will of God, you will receive what he has promised.

Hebrews 12:1

Therefore, since we are surrounded by such a great cloud of witnesses, let us throw off everything that hinders and the sin that so easily entangles. And let us run with perseverance the race marked out for us,

James 1:4

Let perseverance finish its work so that you may be mature and complete, not lacking anything.

PURITY

Lord, create in _____ a pure heart. Help her(him) to stay on the path of purity by living according to Your Word.

Help _____ to see You so her(his) love may abound in knowledge and depth of insight, so she(he) may be able to discern what is best and may be pure and blameless.

Motivate _____ to flee from evil desires. Instead, may she(he) pursue righteousness, faith, love and peace. Help _____ to think about whatever is true, whatever is noble, whatever is right, whatever is pure, whatever is lovely, whatever is admirable. Amen

Scriptures referenced:
Ps. 51:10; Ps. 119:9; Matt. 5:8; Phil. 4:8; 2 Tim. 2:22; James 1:27

Psalm 51:10
Create in me a pure heart, O God, and renew a steadfast spirit within me.

Matthew 5:8
Blessed are the pure in heart, for they will see God.

Philippians 4:8
Finally, brothers and sisters, whatever is true, whatever is noble, whatever is right, whatever is pure, whatever is lovely, whatever is admirable—if anything is excellent or praiseworthy—think about such things.

SELF-CONTROL

L ord, a person without self-control is vulnerable, like a city without walls. Teach ___ to say, "No" to ungodliness and worldly passions, and to live a self-controlled, upright, and godly life.

Help ___ to add to her(his) faith goodness; and to goodness, knowledge; and to knowledge, self-control; and to self-control, perseverance; and to perseverance, godliness; and to godliness, mutual affection; and to mutual affection, love. For if she(he) possesses these qualities in increasing measure, they will keep her(him) from being ineffective and unproductive in her(his) knowledge of God. Amen

Scriptures referenced:
Prov. 16:32; Prov. 25:28; Gal. 5:22-23; Titus 2:11-12; 2 Peter 1:5-8

Proverbs 25:28
Like a city whose walls are broken through is a person who lacks self-control.

Galatians 5:22-23
But the fruit of the Spirit is love, joy, peace, forbearance, kindness, goodness, faithfulness, gentleness and self-control. Against such things there is no law.

Titus 2:11-12
For the grace of God has appeared that offers salvation to all people. It teaches us to say "No" to ungodliness and worldly passions, and to live self-controlled, upright and godly lives in this present age,

SERVANTHOOD

Lord, may _____ serve You with all her(his) heart, soul, mind, and strength. May she(he) observe all Your commands and hold fast to You. May _____ do everything as if she(he) is serving You, not people.

Give _____ eyes see where there is a need. May _____ use the gifts You have given to her(him) to serve and meet the needs of others.

May _____ be eager to serve, not lording it over others, but being a good example and a good steward of Your grace. Amen

Scriptures referenced:
Deut. 10:12-13; Deut. 13:4; Eph. 6:7-8; 1 Peter 4:10-11; 1 Peter 5:2-3

Deuteronomy 13:4
It is the LORD your God you must follow, and him you must revere. Keep his commands and obey him; serve him and hold fast to him.

Ephesians 6:7-8
Serve wholeheartedly, as if you were serving the Lord, not people, because you know that the Lord will reward each one for whatever good they do, whether they are slave or free.

1 Peter 4:10
Each of you should use whatever gift you have received to serve others, as faithful stewards of God's grace in its various forms.

SINCERITY

Lord, may _____ be free of deceit, hypocrisy, and falseness. May she(he) be earnest and genuine in all she(he) does.

May _____'s love be sincere. May she(he) hate what is evil and cling to what is good.

May _____ purify herself(himself) by obeying the truth, so she(he) may have sincere love for others from the heart.

May _____ draw near to You with a sincere heart. May she(he) know the full assurance and freedom from a guilty conscience that faith in You brings. Amen

Scriptures referenced:
Rom. 12:9; 1 Tim. 1:5; Heb. 10; 22; James 3:17; 1 Peter 1:22

Romans 12:9

Love must be sincere. Hate what is evil; cling to what is good.

1 Timothy 1:5

The goal of this command is love, which comes from a pure heart and a good conscience and a sincere faith.

Hebrews 10:22

Let us draw near to God with a sincere heart and with the full assurance that faith brings, having our hearts sprinkled to cleanse us from a guilty conscience and having our bodies washed with pure water.

STEADFASTNESS

Continually renew a steadfast spirit within _____.
May she(he) know the joy of Your salvation and
have a willing spirit to sustain her(him).

May _____ give careful thought to all her(his)
actions so she(he) can be steadfast in obeying all Your
decrees.

You will keep in perfect peace those whose minds
are steadfast, because they trust in you. Help _____ to
trust in You.

May _____ be firm and unwavering in her(his)
faith. Amen

Scriptures referenced:
Ps. 51:10-12; Ps. 119:5; Prov. 4:26; Is. 26:3

Psalm 51:10

Create in me a pure heart, O God, and renew a steadfast spirit within me.

Proverbs 4:26

Give careful thought to the paths for your feet and be steadfast in all your ways.

Isaiah 26:3

You will keep in perfect peace those whose minds are steadfast, because they trust in you.

THANKFULNESS

Lord, may _____ enter Your gates with thanksgiving and Your courts with praise.

May _____ live her(his) life rooted and built up in You, strengthened in faith and overflowing with thankfulness. May Your peace rule her(his) heart.

May_____ devote herself(himself) to prayer, being watchful and thankful, worshipping You with reverence and awe. Amen

Scriptures referenced:
Ps. 100:4; Col. 2:6-7; Col. 3:15; Col. 4:2; Heb. 12:28

Psalm 100:4
Enter his gates with thanksgiving and his courts with praise; give thanks to him and praise his name.

Colossians 3:15
Let the peace of Christ rule in your hearts, since as members of one body you were called to peace. And be thankful.

Colossians 4:2
Devote yourselves to prayer, being watchful and thankful.

WISDOM

Teach _____ the knowledge and good judgment, which comes from trusting Your commands. Help _____ store up Your Word in her(his) heart so she(he) will understand what is right and just and fair. May _____'s wisdom yield patience that allows her(him) to overlook an offense and take action based on wise advice.

May _____ be quick to ask You for wisdom when she(he) needs it. May the wisdom she(he) gains be first of all pure; then peace-loving, considerate, submissive, full of mercy and good fruit, impartial and sincere.

May _____'s understanding of Your ways result in a good life and deeds done in humility. Amen

Scriptures referenced:
Ps. 111:10; Ps. 119:66; Prov. 2:1-2,5,9-10,20; Prov. 13:10; Prov. 19:11; James 1:5, James 3:13,17

Psalm 111:10
The fear of the LORD is the beginning of wisdom; all who follow his precepts have good understanding. To him belongs eternal praise.

James 1:5
If any of you lacks wisdom, you should ask God, who gives generously to all without finding fault, and it will be given to you.

James 3:13, 17
Who is wise and understanding among you? Let them show it by their good life, by deeds done in the humility that comes from wisdom.

Appendix

Commentary on Prayer and Tips for Praying Powerfully & Effectively

FAITHFUL IN PRAYER

When I looked up prayer in the dictionary it had nine definitions. None seemed entirely satisfactory on their own. They used words like, "devout petition" and "spiritual communion with God." There is a reason why it seems nebulous. Prayer is not a simple thing to define because prayer is more than a way to ask God for the things we need or something to turn to only in a crisis. Prayer is a key foundation for an ongoing, full, and abundant relationship with God.

A strong relationship requires healthy communication. Communication makes use of speech, writing, signs, or body language. It is an intricate and complex process. Consequently, because prayer is about relationship with God it shares some of the complexities of healthy communication. Just as there are skills we can learn to become more effective communicators, there are also things we can learn about how to be more powerful and effective in prayer.

God hears the prayers of every person: the just and the unjust, the righteous and the unrighteous. He always answers according to His will with the intent of accomplishing His ultimate purposes. Prayer can be powerful and effective.

The prayer of a righteous person is powerful and effective. James 5:16

A righteous person is always moral and virtuous in their behavior. Does this describe you? If you said no, you are not alone. You are no different than the rest of us. Romans 3:23 tells us "…all have sinned and fall short of the glory of God."

Thanks be to God, He did not abandon or reject us. "…the righteousness of God has been made known, … This righteousness is given through faith in Jesus Christ to all who believe." (Rom. 3:21-22)

If you have placed your faith in Jesus as your personal savior, you received that righteousness. Faith in Jesus restores us to a right standing with God.

"God made him who had no sin to be sin for us, so that in him we might become the righteousness of God." 2 Corinthians 5:21

"For it is by grace you have been saved, through faith— and this is not from yourselves, it is the gift of God— not by works, so that no one can boast." Ephesians 2:8-9

Since our righteousness is not based on works, but on God's grace through faith in Jesus, we can be powerful and effective when we pray, just as it says in James 5:16.

A MODEL FOR PRAYER

Many models for prayer have four parts: praise, confession, thanksgiving, and intercession. Another popular acronym is ACTS: adoration, confession, thanksgiving, and supplication. Each part has a role and a purpose. We will look at each part in detail as we move forward.

Praise

Praise draws us into God's presence. Praise silences the enemy. Praise encourages unity, God-centeredness, and confidence. Praise is like paying compliments to God about the truth of who He is and what He has done.

Confession

Confession allows us to remove any barriers sin places between us and to discern and experience the Holy Spirit's guidance and power.

Thanksgiving

Thanksgiving encourages our faith and confidence in God when we thank Him for His blessings and answered prayer in our lives.

Intercession

Intercession allows us to approach God for the needs and desires of others and ourselves, knowing that He will give us anything we ask that is in accordance with His will.

The Role of Praise and Thanksgiving

The praise portion of the model encourages us to focus on God's character and truths about who He is. The thanksgiving time is focused on thanking Him for answered prayer and the things He has done for us. Even though they are presented separately in many models of prayer with a slightly different focus for each, their purpose and power are essentially the same.

Here are some commands found in the Bible related to praise and thanksgiving.

We are commanded to do it continually.

> "Through Jesus, therefore, let us continually offer to God a sacrifice of praise—the fruit of lips that confess His name." Hebrews 13:15

We are commanded to do it in all circumstances.

> "Be joyful always; pray continually; give thanks in all circumstances, for this is God's will for you in Christ Jesus." 1 Thessalonians 5:16-18

We are to praise and give thanks continuously and in all circumstances. We know two things based on these commands. Praise and thanksgiving are more than just singing worship songs. They cannot be based on emotion alone, if we are to do them in all circumstances. Our emotions will be all over the map: happy, sad, calm, angry, peaceful, scared, patient, frustrated – to name a few. If we only praise and thank God when we feel good, we will miss out on the benefits of their power.

Praise can be like paying compliments to God. A compliment is more meaningful, sincere, and genuine when it includes a specific example of a character trait, skill, or talent of the person to whom you pay the compliment. A compliment should affirm something true about the person. Likewise, verbal praise of God is richer when it includes specifics. However, praise is more than words and songs. Praise happens anytime we profess and affirm the Truth of God through what we think, say, or do. This is why we can be commanded to do it continually.

If praise and thanksgiving are more than sharing good feelings with God, what can praise and thanksgiving accomplish besides making us feel good?

Four things: Access, Unity, God-centeredness, and Confidence

Provides Access to God

In the Old Testament, sacrifices were required to enter God's presence. Jews were only allowed to enter the inner court of the Temple after making numerous, proper sacrifices. The farther into the temple one could go, the fewer the number of people who were allowed. It was narrowed down until only the High Priest was able to proceed behind the curtain that separated the Holy Place from the Most Holy Place, where God's presence dwelt. These sacrifices were called, "atoning sacrifices." Their purpose was to make atonement for the sins of the people. Atonement means to make amends or compensation for a wrong or injury. When Jesus took His last breath on the cross, the curtain in the Temple was torn in two from top to bottom. It was a symbol of our change in status.

> "Now, through Jesus and faith in Him we may approach God with freedom and confidence." Ephesians 3:12

Now, praise becomes our "sacrifice" because it acknowledges the atoning sacrifice of Jesus on our behalf.

> "Through Jesus, therefore let us continually offer God a sacrifice of praise—the fruit of lips that confess His name." Hebrews 13:15

That sacrifice of praise allows us to enter confidently and freely, straight into the presence of God. It provides God with freer access to our hearts and minds as we affirm His Truths. Being in His presence makes us more available to the Holy Spirit. It cultivates and increases our ability to listen and hear the Holy Spirit's guidance.

"Enter His gates with thanksgiving and His courts with praise." Psalm 100:4

Limits the Enemy's Access

Our lives have both a physical and a spiritual dimension. The physical dimension includes what we experience with our five senses. The spiritual dimension has to do with our inner self: our mind, emotions and will. There are both physical and spiritual influences on our lives.

We have spiritual enemies that work to undermine the accomplishment of God's purposes for our lives. Through Jesus' death, resurrection, and the Holy Spirit's presence within us, we have access to spiritual armor that protects us. Praying in the Spirit on all occasions with all kinds of prayers and requests is how we take up the armor of God and stand firm. (Eph. 6:10-18)

Our spiritual enemy is real and he is a liar and a tempter. Prayer and praise work together with the armor of God to provide protection from temptation.

"…you will call your walls salvation and your gates praise." Isaiah 60:18

"The name of the Lord is a fortified tower; the righteous run to it and are safe." Proverbs 18:10

The purpose of city walls and towers was safety. One of the benefits of access into God's presence is safety. The way inside the safety of God's "walls and towers" is through the gates of praise.

Our faith, expressed through praise, provides us with a way to silence the enemy, extinguishes his flaming arrows, and limits his access to us.

"From the lips of children and infants you have ordained praise because of your enemies, to silence the foe and the avenger." Psalm 8:2

Silencing the enemy cleans up the spiritual environment in which you, and those you pray for, make your free will choices. It is worth noting that we don't even need to have the maturity of an adult to be able to use praise to silence the enemy. Even a child can put this power to use.

Fosters Unity

When we start with a focus on thankfulness and praise during prayer times together, it fosters unity. We are drawn together and united around our common faith. If we start from a place of focus on the commonalities of our faith, we can overcome struggles and problems in our relationships. One of Jesus' desires for us is that we "may be built up until we all reach unity in the faith and in the knowledge of the Son of God and become mature, attaining to the whole measure of the fullness of Christ." (Ephesians 4:12-13) One of the things that helps us experience that unity and maturity is praying together in praise and thanksgiving to God.

Fosters God-Centeredness

When we only focus on our problems and desires, we are centered on ourselves instead of God. If we pray to impress others and draw attention to ourselves it will undermine the effectiveness of our prayers. (Luke 18:9-14, Matt. 6:5) When we engage in praise and thanksgiving, we put our focus on God instead of ourselves. That shift in perspective can re-prioritize our desires and help us find solutions and the power to solve problems and resist temptation. Praise and thanksgiving encourage God-centeredness.

Fosters Confidence

Praise and thanksgiving give us confidence in God. They remind us of who God is and all He has done for us. In the Old Testament, God institutionalized worship through Passover, the Harvest Festival, and other Jewish holidays. This was done so His people would not forget His faithfulness. So too, when we engage in praise and thanksgiving it reminds us of His faithfulness. Expressing the truth about God encourages our faith. When our faith is encouraged, it helps us to trust God and wait expectantly for His answers. When our faith is encouraged it releases power. Paul describes the power for those who believe as comparable to the mighty power that raised Jesus from the dead. (Eph. 1:19-20)

Praise and thanksgiving provide access to God, limit the enemy's access to us, and fosters unity, God-centeredness, and confidence. Someone once told me that they felt many people squandered and wasted their worship by focusing on their feelings without taking advantage of and making use of its power. We do not want to be squanderers and wasters. We want to be intentional and strategic in using the power of praise and thanksgiving.

Our Lord is worthy of praise. Praising Him for who He is and standing in the shelter of His shield of faith is the perfect starting place for prayer.

The Role of Confession

"If I had cherished sin in my heart, the Lord would not have listened; but God has surely listened and has heard my prayer. Praise be to God, who has not rejected my prayer or withheld his love from me!" Psalm 66:18-20

When we accept Christ, we receive forgiveness for all our sins. (Acts 13:38-39, 1 Jn. 1:9) We are a new creation, free to choose not to walk according to the flesh but according to the Holy Spirit that dwells within us. However, none of us is completely mature in Christ, so we still succumb to our sinful desires. If we leave those sins unconfessed, it is like allowing a pile of rubble to build up, making a barrier between us and the ability to discern the Holy Spirit's guidance and power. When we confess our sins, their power as a barrier is swept away and we are completely free to live by the Spirit.

There is a reason why praise comes before confession. The enemy wants to heap condemnation on us for our sins. Condemnation leads to shame and feelings of failure and disgrace. It encourages hopelessness and leads to apathy and a lack of growth or positive change. Praise has the power to silence the enemy's condemnation. (Ps.8:2)

The Holy Spirit will convict us of our sin. However, this conviction does not come with condemnation. (Rom. 8:1-2) The Holy Spirit's conviction leads to repentance and forgiveness. Repentance is defined: "to feel such sorrow for sin or fault as to be disposed to change one's life for the better."[2] Notice that this conviction leads to turning away from the sin and towards the experience of forgiveness and grace through Jesus. The experience of conviction by the Holy Spirit leads towards positive change. When we spend time in praise before confession, we silence the enemy's condemnation and are open to the appropriate, life changing conviction of the Holy Spirit.

The Role of Intercession

Intercession is a prayer to God on behalf of the needs of others and ourselves. We can freely bring all our requests and anxieties to God. (1 Pet. 5:7)

"Do not be anxious about anything, but in every situation, by prayer and petition, with thanksgiving, present your requests to God." Philippians 4:6

He desires for us to carry each other's burdens. (Gal. 6:2) We can only be in one place at a time, so prayer becomes one of our most effective ways to carry those burdens. When we bring everything to God in prayer, He promises to "meet all our needs according to the riches of His glory in Christ Jesus." (Phil. 4:19)

Whatever We Ask

There are verses in the Bible that say we can have whatever we ask for in prayer. However, just as there are conditions you have to meet to receive a good grade in a class, there are some conditions for receiving whatever you ask in prayer. It starts with the righteousness we receive through the forgiveness of our sins when we put our faith in Jesus. Here are some others found in scripture.

James 1:6 tells us, "when you ask, you must believe and not doubt, because the one who doubts is like a wave of the sea, blown and tossed by the wind." Doubt can be overcome when you choose, like Abraham, to believe that God is able to do what He promises. (Romans 4:20-21) Faith is not a feeling. It is something we can choose in spite of how we may feel.

James 4:1-3 tells us we do not have because we do not ask and that we do not receive when we ask with wrong motives.

James 5:13-16 tells us that prayer offered in faith combined with confessing our sins will be powerful and effective.

Notice how praise and confession, coming before intercession, help eliminate some of the obstacles to our powerful and effective prayers. Praise encourages our faith and sweeps away doubt by reminding us of the truth. Confession helps us set aside and avoid wrong motives.

In **John 15** Jesus talks about the importance of remaining in Him. He compares us to the branches on a vine that need to remain in the vine in order to bear fruit. Then, in verses 7-16, Jesus says if we remain in Him and His words remain in us we will receive whatever we ask.

In **1 John 5:14-15** we find a final condition for receiving whatever we ask.

"This is the confidence we have in approaching God: that if we ask anything according to his will, he hears us. And if we know that he hears us—whatever we ask— we know that we have what we asked of him."
1 John 5:14-15

To receive whatever we ask for in prayer, it must be according to God's will. This is actually a freeing thing. It means we can safely ask God about any concern or desire of our heart without the fear of asking for or receiving the wrong thing. He will only give us what is according to His will.

Praying Using Scriptures

Praying the truth by using the Word of God has great power and brings life in unique and powerful ways.

"His Word is a lamp to our feet and a light to our path." Psalm 119:105

Isaiah 55:10-11 says,

"As the rain and the snow come down from heaven, and do not return to it without watering the earth and making it bud and flourish, so that it yields seed for the sower and bread for the eater, so is my word that goes out from my mouth: It will not return to me empty, but will accomplish what I desire and achieve the purpose for which I sent it."

God's Word not only accomplishes its purposes, but it also has the power to set us free. John 17:17 tells us God's Word is truth and John 8:32 tells us the truth will set us free. When Ephesians 6:12-18 describes the whole armor of God, the sword of the Spirit is clearly identified as the Word of God. It is the only piece of the armor of God that is actually a weapon. Immediately following the identification of the sword of the Spirit comes the direction in verse 18, "to pray in the Spirit on all occasions with all kinds of prayers." Praying in the Spirit and using the Truth of God's Word, is a powerful and effective weapon of spiritual warfare. It is a form of blessing to the people for whom you pray. It can bring healing, freedom, and strength.

Using scripture to pray helps align us with God's will. We know from the scriptures that we receive whatever we ask that is according to God's will. Praying using scripture is not a 100 percent guarantee that we are praying according to God's will. It is possible to use scripture out of context. People have been known to twist scriptures to serve their own purposes, not God's. However, using scripture to pray greatly increases the likelihood of what we ask being according to God's will.

Examples of Scripture Prayers

Some scriptures are already prayers, which makes it easy. Here is an example of a scripture prayer.

Romans 15:5-6

"May the God who gives endurance and encouragement give you the same attitude of mind toward each other that Christ Jesus had, so that with one mind and one voice you may glorify the God and Father of our Lord Jesus Christ." Amen

You can use the content of a verse and create a prayer. Here are some examples.

Isaiah 41:13

"For I am the LORD your God who takes hold of your right hand and says to you, do not fear; I will help you."

Prayer

May _____ know that You are his(her) God, who takes hold of his(her) right hand and says to him(her), "Do not fear; I will help you." Amen

2 Thessalonians 2:15

"So then, brothers and sisters, stand firm and hold to the teachings we passed on to you, whether by word of mouth or by letter."

Prayer

Lord Jesus, help ___ to stand firm and hold to things he(she) has been taught from Your Word. Amen

GOD LINKS HIS ACTIONS
WITH OUR PRAYERS

Sometimes I wonder why God chose to link His actions with our praying. Due to free will, sometimes God waits to be asked and to be invited to act. He has established our prayers as a powerful influence on how and when He meets our physical, emotional, and spiritual needs. Ruth Meyers, in *Thirty-One Days of Prayer*[3], suggests it is because of His desire to be in relationship with us. Prayer keeps us aware of Him as our source, links our lives with God's exciting purposes and power, and roots us in how much we need and depend on Him. Even if we don't pray, He still holds everything together, is the source of every good thing, and accomplishes His ultimate purposes.

S.D. Gordon, a well-known devotional writer, wrote:

"The great people of the earth today are the people who pray. I do not mean those who talk about prayer; nor those who say they believe in prayer; nor yet those who can explain about prayer; but I mean those people whom take time and pray. They have not time. It must be taken from something else. This something else is important, and pressing, but still less important and less pressing than prayer."[4]

Prayer is an incredible gift Jesus gave us when He enabled us to come freely and confidently into the presence of God. Whenever we take time to intercede in prayer for God's people and purposes we release His power on our behalf.

WHAT IF WE DON'T KNOW WHAT TO PRAY?

We all struggle with knowing how to pray sometimes.

"In the same way, the Spirit helps us in our weakness. We do not know what we ought to pray for. But the Spirit himself intercedes for us through wordless groans. And he who searches our hearts knows the mind of the Spirit, because the Spirit intercedes for God's people in accordance with the will of God." Romans 8:26-27

"But because Jesus lives forever, he has a permanent priesthood. Therefore, he is able to save completely those who come to God through him, because he always lives to intercede for them." Hebrews 7:24-25

When we don't know what to pray, we can always stand in agreement with what the Holy Spirt and Jesus request for the people or situations for which we intercede. These kinds of moments are also a time when you can turn to scripture to help you pray.

What if we know what we would like to pray, but we just don't know how? I was once asked why I didn't just ask God to heal someone without being formal and wordy in how I prayed. My friend would have preferred me to just say, "God, please heal her broken bone. Amen." We absolutely can ask God very directly for things. As a matter of fact, it is a good idea to ask God for exactly what our hopes and desires are for the people we pray for and for ourselves. After all, we are told in James 4:2-3 that we do not have because we do not ask God.

We are to use our intelligence and creative imaginations combined with our knowledge of God's principles and promises when we pray. God cares more about the integrity of our relationship with Him and the motives of our heart than about the actual words we use. Formal or informal, wordy or brief, God wants to hear it all. We can boldly ask for things for ourselves and others because God is trustworthy. He knows our hearts and our needs and the hearts and needs of the people for whom we pray. He will answer according to His will.

RAISE YOUR HANDS
TO THE LORD

Here is the story of Israel's defeat of the Amalekites from Exodus 17:8-14.

"The Amalekites attacked the Israelites at Rephidim. Moses said to Joshua, "Choose some of our men and go out to fight the Amalekites. Tomorrow, I will stand on top of the hill with the staff of God in my hands." Therefore, Joshua fought the Amalekites as Moses had ordered, and Moses, Aaron, and Hur accompanied him to the top of the hill. As long as Moses held up his hands, the Israelites won, but whenever he lowered his hands, the Amalekites won.

When Moses' hands grew tired, they took a stone and put it under him and he sat on it. Aaron and Hur held his hands up - one on one side, one on the other - so that his hands remained steady till sunset. Joshua overcame the Amalekite army with the sword. Then the Lord said to Moses, "Write this on a scroll as something to be remembered and make sure that Joshua hears it, because I will completely blot out the name of Amalek from under heaven."

In this story of Israel's battle with the Amalekites, we have a physical demonstration of a spiritual reality.

Every aspect of our lives has a spiritual dimension. That spiritual dimension is a critical dynamic that permeates the fabric of our lives. The battle with the Amalekites could not have been won without Joshua and his men going out to fight. It equally could not have been won without the spiritual intercession of Moses, Aaron, and Hur. Raised hands were a symbol of appealing to God for help and enablement. As long as Moses' hands were raised to God, the Israelites were winning. When his hands came down, the Amalekites were winning. When he became weary, Aaron and Hur came alongside to support him until the battle was won. Moses provided right leadership, but the battle would not have been won without Aaron and Hur's support.

This story is rich with lessons about the interdependence of the physical and spiritual dimensions and our complete dependence on God to help and enable the accomplishment of the work God has prepared for us to do. Like Joshua and his men, we all have physical jobs to do. When we take time to pray, we take on the spiritual role of Moses, Aaron, and Hur. We can enlist the help and enablement of God on our behalf and on behalf of the mission to become all God intends. Just as the support of Aaron and Hur was critical to the defeat of the Amalekites, our prayers are critical to the success of our missions.

WALLS AND WATCHMEN

"I looked for someone among them who would build up the wall and stand before me in the gap on behalf of the land so I would not have to destroy it, but I found no one. So, I will pour out my wrath on them and consume them with my fiery anger, bringing down on their own heads all they have done, declares the Sovereign Lord." Ezekiel 22:30-31

These verses are commonly interpreted to be a call for watchmen to serve as intercessors in prayer on behalf of the people. The prophets, such as Ezekiel, were sent to be watchmen for the people, to warn them and dissuade them from evil. Walls were a main source of protection for a city. When there were gaps in the wall the city was vulnerable. Gaps needed to be watched over and guarded until they could be repaired. They are a physical example of a spiritual reality. When you pray for others, you build up the walls and stand in the gap between them and the spiritual forces of evil that strive to undermine the accomplishment of God's purposes. You protect and further God's work whenever you make time to pray. When God looked for someone in Ezekiel's time he found no one, but when he looks at the people you pray for he finds you among those who stand. When you take time to pray, you make a powerful and effective difference in their lives.

Thwart the Enemy's Schemes

Stand in the gap on behalf of others.
Stand firm, putting on the full armor of God.

"Take up the shield of faith with which you can extinguish the flaming arrows of the evil one." Ephesians 6:16

"Through the praises of children and infants you have established a stronghold against your enemies to silence the foe and the avenger." Psalm 8:2

STAND FIRM ON BEHALF OF OTHERS

"Epaphras is always wrestling in prayer for you, that you may stand firm in all the will of God, mature and fully assured." Colossians 4:12

When God created us, it was so important to Him that our love be freely given to Him that He gave us free will. Free will meant we had the freedom to reject Him. Which, ultimately and unfortunately, we did. That rejection brought brokenness into the world at every level. That brokenness requires justice and healing. God chose to send Jesus to pay the price for justice, so we might have an eternity in heaven with Him. Through Jesus' death and resurrection, victory was accomplished once for all.

However, in the physical realm He did not eliminate the consequences of brokenness. The Holy Spirit works within us to redeem something of value from them. He is present with us as we deal with living in a broken world until our lives here come to an end and we receive the ultimate healing of a new body in a new heaven and a new earth.

Free will also means that we cannot use prayer to force someone to take a particular action. They have free will to believe or behave however they want. Just as we saw in the story of Israel's victory over the Amalekites. All of our lives are lived under the influence of the spiritual realm. While we cannot force anyone, we have great power through prayer over the spiritual environment in which they make their choices.

Paul tells us we should stand firm against the spiritual forces of evil. Because of Jesus' victory, we have power in the spiritual realm to stand firm, silencing the enemy of our souls so that choices can be freely made based on the truth. God looks for people who are willing to stand firm in prayer on behalf of others.

> "You too, be patient and stand firm, because the Lord's coming is near." James 5:8

STAND UP, FOR, IN

Up – Against Satan's Schemes

Stand up against Satan's schemes, to undermine the accomplishment of God's purposes. Eph. 6:11-18 encourages us to put on the full armor of God, which includes the shield of faith, with which we can extinguish the flaming arrows of the evil one.

For - The Mighty Work of the Holy Spirit

Stand for the mighty work of the Holy Spirit, who dwells in our hearts. Phil. 3:13 tells us that it is God who works in us to will and to act according to His good purpose. Paul prays for us to know God's great power for those who believe. It is the same power that raised Jesus from the dead.

In – Agreement with the Holy Spirit's Intercessions

Stand in agreement with what the Holy Spirit intercedes for us. Rom. 8:26-27 tells us that when we do not know what to pray for, the Holy Spirit knows our hearts and intercedes for God's people in accordance with the Will of God.

Even though our own strength is inadequate, when we stand up against Satan's schemes we align ourselves with God's invincible power to overcome. When we pray for the mighty work of the Holy Spirit, it reminds us that the work is spiritual not just physical in nature. Standing in agreement with the Spirit's intercessions aligns us in submission to God's will.

Praying this three-step pattern lacks specificity. Of course, its effectiveness soars when it is combined with worship, confession, obedience, and specifics. However, in less than a minute, you will have aligned yourselves with the invincible power of God, invited the work of the Holy Spirit, and placed yourselves in agreement with God's will. It is a powerful return on a moments investment.

Perseverance Produces a Crop

Jesus told his disciples a parable in Luke 18 to show them that they should always pray and not give up. It was the story of a persistent widow who kept pleading with a judge for justice until he finally gave in and gave it to her. If an evil judge will eventually respond to perseverance, how much more will our loving Heavenly Father respond to our perseverance in prayer?

Perseverance is important in many aspects of our lives. Romans 5:1-5 reminds us that perseverance brings about proven character. James 1:2-4 tells us perseverance's work is to make us mature and complete, not lacking anything.

In 2 Peter 1:3-8, perseverance is in the center of a list of qualities whose possession in increasing measure will keep us from being ineffective and unproductive in our knowledge of our Lord Jesus Christ.

Perseverance is central to the production of a crop in the Parable of the Sower. "But the seed on good soil stands for those with a noble and good heart, who hear the word, retain it, and by perseverance, produce a crop." (Luke 8:15) In the Parable of the Sower, the good soil is described in these ways:

One who hears the Word
One who accepts the Word
One who understands the Word
One who has a noble and good heart
One, who by perseverance, produces a crop a hundred, sixty, or thirty times what was sown

When we persevere together in prayer, we can look forward to a great harvest in God's economy. "Let us not become weary in doing good, for at the proper time we will reap a harvest if we do not give up." (Galatians 6:9)

Be Powerful and Effective

We have looked at some of the purposes and roles prayer plays in our lives and why God would call us to do it continuously. My hope is that you will become increasingly strategic in how you pray.

> "Come and hear, all you who fear God; let me tell you what He has done for me. I cried out to Him with my mouth; His praise was on my tongue. If I had cherished sin in my heart, the Lord would not have listened; but God has surely listened and has heard my prayer. Praise be to God, who has not rejected my prayer or withheld his love from me." Psalm 66:16-20

Since we are so blessed, let us not grow weary or lose heart.

> "Let us run with perseverance the race marked out for us, fixing our eyes on Jesus, the pioneer and perfecter of faith." Hebrews 12:1-2

> "Let us not become weary in doing good, for at the proper time we will reap a harvest if we do not give up." Galatians 6:9

NOTES

1. Anne Arkins & Gary Harrell. Watchman on the Walls: Praying Character into Your Child. Sisters,Oregon. Multnomah Publishers. 1996
2. Dictionary.com,LCC. (2010). Dictionary.com (version 7.2.1) [mobile application software]. Retrieved from http://appstore.apple.com
3. Warren & Ruth Myers. 31 Days of Prayer: Moving God's Mighty Hand. Sisters, Oregon. Multnomah Publishing. 1997
4. Gordon, S.D. Quiet Talks on Prayer. New York. Grosset & Dunlap. 1904

ORDER INFORMATION

To order additional copies of this book, please visit
www.redemption-press.com.
Also available on Amazon.com and BarnesandNoble.com
Or by calling toll free 1-844-2REDEEM.

CPSIA information can be obtained
at www.ICGtesting.com
Printed in the USA
LVHW051222141020
668673LV00006B/646